YOUR KNOWLEDGE HAS VALUE

Bibliographic information published by the German National Library:

The German National Library lists this publication in the National Bibliography; detailed bibliographic data are available on the Internet at http://dnb.dnb.de .

Imprint:

Copyright © 2011 GRIN Verlag, Open Publishing GmbH
Print and binding: Books on Demand GmbH, Norderstedt Germany
ISBN: 9783668530911

This book at GRIN:

http://www.grin.com/en/e-book/373214/trade-relations-between-the-eu-and-developing-countries

Benjamin Lueber

Trade Relations between the EU and Developing Countries

Have the Trade Policies of the EU contributed to the External Constraints which hamper the Development in the South?

GRIN Publishing

GRIN - Your knowledge has value

Since its foundation in 1998, GRIN has specialized in publishing academic texts by students, college teachers and other academics as e-book and printed book. The website www.grin.com is an ideal platform for presenting term papers, final papers, scientific essays, dissertations and specialist books.

Visit us on the internet:

http://www.grin.com/

http://www.facebook.com/grincom

http://www.twitter.com/grin_com

Trade relations between the EU and developing countries

Have the Trade Policies of the EU contributed to the External Constraints which hamper the Development in the South?

Benjamin Lüber
1/28/2011

Introduction

The countries located on the African continent continue to be marginalized in the world economic system. In contrast to regions such as East Asia and Latin America, which in the last decades have shown their potential to decrease poverty and join the ranks of the developed world in the future, the prospects for African states, and especially the states of Sub-Saharan Africa (SSA), remain remarkably bleak. The various indications of this dire state need not be repeated here, as they are presented in every textbook addressing the economic situation of the Third World, such as in *Understanding Third World Politics* (Smith, B.C., 2009).

As there may be a consensus on the lack of development in Sub-Saharan Africa, this is far from true when it comes to understanding the causes of this lack of development. The scientific study that concerns itself not only with analyzing the root causes of this lack of development, but also with providing recommendations for how economic development can be achieved is called development economics. Diana Hunt set as her objective to outline the main perspectives, which all approach development economics differently. She distinguished between six major perspectives: the structuralist-, neo-Marxist-, Maoist-, basic needs-, neo-classical paradigms and dependency analyses (1989). A very important part in the debates between them has been on the question whether internal, i.e. "domestic mism anagement", or external influences, i.e. "the structure of the global economy", lay at the basis of the mal-performance of African states (Clapham, 1996, p. 812). It goes without saying that developing a better understanding of the *real* causes that constrain African development is a crucial element towards economic progress on this continent. In this thesis, the theoretical perspective of dependency theory will be applied.

Trade policy of the European Union towards the states of the South provides an example of such external influences. In short, since the gaining of independence of former colonial countries the developed countries have used trade policy as a means to restrict the access of their products to their markets (Rittberger, 2006, p. 178). These restrictions have differed to various degrees, but on the face of it, the purpose has been to protect sensitive industries in which developing countries possessed a comparative advantage (DeVault, 1996, p. 35). There has been a growing realization that liberalization of the markets of developed economies for goods from developing countries is an important pre-requisite for their development. Without such changes, other "testimonies" of a will to aid developing countries, i.e. development aid, can be seen as nothing more but cosmetics (Rittberger, 2006, p.178).

Assessing the degree to which trade policy inhibits economic progress of developing countries requires a closer look at how trade policy has manifested itself. After the Second World War a liberal international economic order was established and maintained up to the present time. When newly independent nations of SSA entered into trade relations with other countries, these took place within the framework of this liberal order. The General Agreement on Tariffs and Trade (GATT) was the institution that regulated these relations. Members of this organization needed to play according to its rules, of which the most-favoured nation (MFN) principle was the most important. Basically, it means that a country must be non-discriminatory with regard to the tariffs it applies towards other countries. For example, the lowest tariff that is applied on steel must be applied to all trading partners. Developing countries regarded this principle based on reciprocity as limiting their development opportunities, and therefore pressured to change the system by calling for a new international economic order (NIEO) (Sapir et al, 2008, p.207). As we now know, the developed countries proved unwilling to accommodate their proposals. However, developing countries succeeded on one front by being able to introduce an exemption into the rule book of GATT: the Generalized System of Preferences (GSP).

GSP allowed developing countries to negotiate preferential trade agreements (PTA's) with developed countries, making it possible that developed countries granted imports from developing countries preferential tariff treatment. These were non-reciprocal, meaning that lower tariffs on the side of developed countries did not need to be met by the same concession on the side of developing countries. The original intention was to create a generalized system, but it turned out that GSP schemes were introduced by several industrialized countries, at different times (Sapir et al, 2008, p.208). The then European Economic Community was proud to announce its first PTA in 1971 before other industrialized countries followed suit (Faber et al, 2008, p.194). The United States of America (U.S.) were the last country to introduce their GSP in January 1976 (Sapir et al, 2008, p.208). Another pillar of EU trade relations with developing countries is constituted by the EU's association agreements. The first such agreement was unilaterally adopted by the EEC in 1957 upon the coming into force of the Treaty of Rome. The ensuing Yaoundé and Lomé Conventions, and the latest Cotonou Agreement saw the number of developing countries party to these association agreements rising substantially. The African, Caribbean and Pacific Group of States (ACP) that first united surrounding the negotiation of Lomé I in 1975 now consists of 79 developing countries, covering nearly all the states located in Sub-Saharan Africa.

Many studies have confirmed that the GSP have shown not to be of a great economic stimulus for developing countries (DeVault, 1996, p.35). The effectiveness of the GSP in contributing to export earnings of developing countries has been undermined by factors such as non-tariff barriers to trade, limits on preferential treatment and the limited nature of GSP coverage. The GSP scheme of the EU can hardly be seen as standing out as a contribution to a world trade system that is more conducive to developing countries. Concerning the EU's association agreements, observers have been less critical. Especially the first Lomé Convention was hailed by some as constituting an agreement that gives important concessions to developing countries (Frey-Wouters, 1980, p.3).

In the broader relationship between dominant economies of the North, and the economies of the South, how should the external influence that the EU has on developing countries be viewed? Some economic theories, especially the more radical ones, have brought forward arguments to explain how the North is underdeveloping the South. Dependency theory in particular regards the world capitalist system as an extremely hostile environment that prevents development in the South. Thus, this thesis will evaluate to what extent the external influences of the EU upon the developing countries correspond to the theories of dependency theory concerning underdevelopment.

Since its creation, the EU has incorporated states that are among the most dominant ones in the world economic system. Up to now, many states have acceded. Therefore, the EU can be regarded as constituting an important trading bloc. This shows that the EU has always been an important player giving form to the structure of the global economy. Consequently, a study of its trade relations with developing countries is of great value to assess how strong external influences have weighed on the development opportunities of the South. Furthermore, such an examination may be able to contribute to an understanding of how external factors come to affect the global South. Accordingly, the main research question reads as follows: *To what*

3

*extent do trade relations between the EU and developing countries, constituting as
they do an example of external factors influencing the development of developing
countries, validate the assumptions of dependency theory?*

The research question, first of all, necessitates an outline of the m ain tenets of
dependency theory. Thus, the first sub-question w ill be: *How does dependency
theory account for underdevelopment in the South?* The second research question
provides for a closer exam ination of the com position, the details and the evolution of
trade policy between the EU and developing countries. Therefore, the second chapter
w ill address the sub-question: *How has trade policy and development cooperation of
the EU with the developing country manifested itself, and what are the
circumstances under which the trade regimes of the EC towards developing
countries have come into existence?* Based on a better understanding of EU trade
policy, the effect of EU trade on developing countries w ill subsequently be analyzed.
The question that underlies the third chapter is: *Have the trade policies of the EU
contributed to the external constraints which hamper the development of developing
countries?*

Chapter I: The theoretical insights of dependency theory: the ambitious and radical strand of Frank and Amin

This section will deal with the question: *How does dependency theory account for underdevelopment in the South?* To start off, some remarks concerning the coherence of the theoretical perspective that is called dependency theory should be made. These remarks are necessary in order to clarify what particular branch of dependency theory will be scrutinized in the remainder of this thesis. It is widely accepted that dependency theory shares among its different variations two assumptions. First, development of the economies in the South is conditioned because of its dependence on other economies. Second, this dependence is more than the common interdependence in times of globalization because it is structural and goes deeper (Brown, 1985, p.62). Apart from that, however, the views of dependency theorists diverge (Ibid.). Within the academic community there is no consensus on "whether or not several dependency theories exist or can ever exist" (Browett, 1985, p.790). Therefore, it is not possible to speak of a dependency paradigm. Rather, a scholar writing in the late 1980's in the field of economic theories of development regarded dependency theory as constituting not more than the mere seeds of a new paradigm (Hunt, 1989). Twenty years later the situation seems to have remained unchanged.

One reason for the lack of paradigmatic nature can be found in the fact that dependency theory draws from several other theories. Of the several theoretical backgrounds that are identified by Wil Hout I would like to focus shortly on the neo-Marxist background.[1] It seems to me quite striking that André Gunder Frank, who is seen by many as the most influential figure within dependency theory (Foster-Caster, 1976, p.173), was put by Diana Hunt into the neo-Marxist school of thought (Hunt, 1989). Indeed, Frank's work bears a clear Marxist heritage (Brown, 1985, p. 65), although this was always rejected by himself (Hout, 1993, p.54). For example, his theoretical insights rely heavily on those of Baran, a neo-Marxist scholar (Foster-Caster, 1976, pp. 167–168). Furthermore, Samir Amin, who is another important figure within dependency theory, does consider himself as a Marxist. The point that I

5

am trying to make is that it becomes difficult for dependency theory to carve out its own paradigm if some of its scholars show more affinity with other paradigms.

Yet, it is possible to classify dependency theory. In this thesis I will follow the classification of Chris Brown. He regards dependency theory as composed of "dependencia", "centre-periphery analysis" and "world-system analysis" (Brown, 1985). This thesis will mainly rely on the theoretical perspective of those scholars whose work is connected with "centre-periphery analysis". Whereas dependendistas[2] have limited themselves to studying the dependent nature of Latin America, scholars writing on centre-periphery relations include in their studies the whole periphery, which is all developing countries (Brown, 1985, p.65). It might be necessary to recall that this thesis is trying to investigate the causes for underdevelopment of the ACP group of states. Furthermore, this branch of dependency theory is a more "ambitious and radical version of 'dependencia'" (Brown, 1985, p.64), as will become clear later on.

Wil Hout identifies André Gunder Frank, Samir Amin, Giovanni Arrighi and Johan Galtung as the most important writers analyzing centre-periphery relations. The works of Frank and Amin show sufficient similarities, which has led to a tendency to regard these theories, together with Wallerstein's world-system analysis, as constituting the dependency perspective (Browett, 1985, p.790). Thus, when I will be using the term dependency theory or perspective in the remainder of this thesis, this perspective should be regarded as being constituted particularly by the works of Frank and Amin.

The thesis will proceed by outlining the main tenets of this branch of dependency theory, referring to Frank and Amin where the ideas can be directly traced back to them. Frank's first contribution to the study of dependency had wide repercussions, and he may be seen as the figure who increased the influence of dependency by giving it a higher profile (Foster-Caster, 1976, p. 175). This had certainly to do with the fact that Frank's conception of dependency was, as mentioned, more ambitious and radical (Brown, 1985, p.64). To a substantial part the significance of his first contribution stems from his difference between undevelopment and underdevelopment. In his article "the development of

---

[1] The other theoretical backgrounds that are described are traditional economies theories of development, liberal theories, the E.C.L.A. approach and modernization theories. (Hout, 1993, pp.19–38)

[2] Dependendistas are writers within the field of dependencia.

6

underdevelopment" from 1966 he argues that while the now advanced economies of the centre can be regarded as undeveloped prior to industrialization, the state of development in the periphery can be characterized as underdeveloped (Frank, 1964, pp.150-151).

Besides, it should be noted that the centre is composed of the dominant economies of the world system, while the periphery is more or less composed of the developing countries (Hout, 1993, p.78). This is not very specific, and must be seen as a major deficiency of dependency theorists (Disney, 1977, p.126). On the overall, a major criticism of dependency theory is that its propositions are "at a very high level of generality" (Foster-Carter, 1976, p.172).

As the title already states, Frank attributes an active role to the dominant economies in the underdevelopment of the South. This argumentation stands in stark contrast with another influential theory of that time, which is modernization theory. Modernization theory maintains that underdevelopment was due to the dualist nature in developing countries, meaning that for development to take place the still existing pre-capital, sometimes called feudal, production structures needed to be modernized (Hout, 1993, pp.34-38). In contrast, Frank argued that colonization had a profound and lasting effect on the colonies and the whole of its population. Thus, he regards backward areas of the country, and the underdevelopment in general, as the "historical product of past and continuing economic and other relations between the satellite underdeveloped and the now developed metropolitan countries" (Frank, 1994, p.150).

The stress on "continuing economic and other relations" makes clear that dependency has some common ground with "neo-colonialism", as they both insist that political independence of the developing countries has resulted in only limited room for political manoeuvring (Smith, 1979, p.247). Frank and Amin tell us that we must perceive the development possibilities of the South as structurally limited by the place they occupy within the world capitalist system. It is the structure of the international system that is the "key variable to be studied in order to understand the form that development has taken".

Consequently, and this is the main critique of Tony Smith, they totally discard the individual nations of the South as a unit of analysis (1979, p.252). This is because they argue that the nations of the South will, as long as they are part of the global capitalist system, be forced to perform the functions according to their status as a periphery. From this it follows that Frank and Amin maintain that the countries of the South are not able to influence their own affairs. The pressures need to be seen as strong enough to make autonomous decision-making stimulating their own development impossible. Accordingly, Amin and Frank regard it as pointless to analyze specific cases. This position has brought them into a position of unease with regard to the explanation of the good performance of the Newly Industrializing Countries. The dependency theorists needed to defend themselves against the argument that policies did matter (Browett, 1985, pp.789-790). However, their stance remained the same. Amin kept on insisting that it is misleading to analyze specific cases, since these typologies would "mask the underlying unity of the phenomenon of underdevelopment" (Smith, 1980, p.7). To understand that point, it is necessary to examine more closely the nature of the global capitalist system, as perceived by Amin and Frank.

As with Frank's aforementioned title, "accumulation on a world scale" (1974), which is the title of one of Amin's monographs, is already very indicative of the thrust of his analysis. It indicates that the roots of underdevelopment are to be found by an analysis on the world level. Amin and Frank come together in the assumption that the necessities of capital accumulation in the centre prevent development in the periphery. According to Frank, we find the answers to the underdevelopment of the South in the nature of capitalism itself. He states that the logical tail to successful development of capitalism in the centre is the distortion of capitalist development in the periphery. In other words, capitalism makes the economies adjust to the needs of capitalist development in the centre (Frank, 1994, p.153). Thus, a subservient role is established for the periphery. In addition, Amin claims that the pressures of the international capitalist system entail that the economies of the South become extraverted and that their production structures get distorted in order to serve an external market (Amin, 1994, p.162). This is what Frank describes as "satellite status", and he asserts as a kind of rule of thumb that development in the South is limited by this status (Frank, 1994, p.154).

Moreover, he claims that their satellite status is a result of their historical participation in the world capitalist system, which transformed their economic structure into a capitalist export economy. Actually, it is this argumentation on which he builds his difference between underdevelopment and undevelopment. According to Frank, the now-advanced countries could once be described as undeveloped precisely because they have never had the status of a satellite (Frank, 1994, p.154). On the other hand, the distortion of the peripheries' economies has obstructed capitalism from leading to "a full flowering of the capitalist mode of production" there (Amin, 1994, p.162).

I will now go in a little deeper into Amin's argumentation. While the production structure in the centre is "self-centred", it is "externally oriented" in the periphery. In a "self-centred" production structure the domestic mass market for consumer goods and a producer goods sector can flourish. An "externally oriented" system, on the other hand, knows a dominance of the export sector, as well as a strong market for luxury goods (Schiffer, 1981, pp. 516–517). This equals down to balanced development in the centre – "the production of capital goods and goods for mass consumption" – and unbalanced development in the periphery – "the production for export and the production of luxury goods" (Browett, 1985, p. 792). This external orientation, according to Amin, makes the economy dependent, and prevents successful development, since only autocentred development policies are successful (Hout, 1993, p. 76). Most importantly, Amin argues that the high concentration of the export sector in the economy is due to the fact that capitalism in the periphery developed "as a result of external forces" (Schiffer, 1981, p.517). The export sector is stimulated by investments from the centre because investments tend to go where the profits are. The high availability of labour in the periphery leads to a cheap supply of labour, which leads to low production costs (Ibid.).

One might wonder now why these investments do not lead to growth in the periphery? This is where Amin's concept of "unequal exchange" becomes important. "Unequal exchange" implies the transfer of "super-surplus" (Browett, 1985, p.792). The transfer of surplus, as well as other reasons ensure that labour in the periphery will not be able to increase their wages (Schiffer, 1981, p.517). This assumption is inextricably linked with his view that the function of the periphery, "within the international division of labour and commodity production, is to provide the appropriate institutional and productive framework to ensure a continual supply of cheap labour to the export sector" (Schiffer, 1981, p.517). I think that there is a strong connection between the two assumptions because Amin needs to establish that the costs of labour will not rise in order to be able to infer that the periphery is doomed to remain externally oriented.

By now, I think one should be able to understand why scholars like Aidan Foster-Caster depict Frank's formulations as "extremely crude" (1976, p.176). This does not count only for Frank, but also for Amin. Both operate on a high level of generality, and completely refrain from providing reasons for "why, how and under what conditions underdevelopment has been, and still remains, a necessary and inevitable consequence of what they define as capitalism" (Browett, 1985, p.793). Their focus on capitalism as the main explanatory force is clearly exaggerated. The crude nature of their theoretical perspectives is also evident in their refusal to analyze specific cases. For example, how should we treat countries like Portugal, Greece, Brazil and Argentina? The former two countries have never been colonized, whereas the latter two have been. Nevertheless, we still can find many similarities between the countries regarding their economic nature. Capitalist industry in both Argentina and Portugal is similarly limited and backward (Disney, 1977, p.126).

To top the point, the political strategy that both recommend to peripheral countries seems far-fetched. Namely, both conclude that the only viable option for development to take place is to choose the socialist path (Schiffer, 1981, p.518). In other words, a complete and radical break of ties with the centre is the only way to escape the dilemma (Smith, 1980, p.20). Summarizing, an important critique towards the works of Amin and Frank is that their propositions are not fully thought through, or unsubstantiated (Ibid.)

Chapter II: Evolution of EU trade policy and its circum stances

This section will deal with the circum stances under which the trade regim es of the EC towards developing countries have com e into existence, and their developm ent up to the present trade relations between the EU and developing countries.[1] This will be done with keeping in m ind the question of whether these trade regim es have contributed to a world trade system that is conducive to the developm ent of countries in the South. In that regard, it is im portant to note that on at least two occasions the EC has proudly proclaim ed the introduction of trade regim es due to its alleged advantages for developing countries. Firstly, the EC regarded itself as a forerunner of the industrialized world when it adopted in 1971 as the first industrialized trading bloc its Generalized System of Preferences (GSP). The U S., for exam ple, only followed suit in 1976. The second tim e it did so was at the conclusion of the Lom é Convention in 1975. The EC felt that it had established a trade agreem ent that was exceptional in nature when seen in the light of an international econom ic order that gave little beneficial treatm ent to the special needs and dem ands of developing countries. Claude Cheysson, who was a m em ber of the EC Com m ission responsible for developm ent and cooperation, put it in the following words: "All this work has produced an agreem ent which, I say with som e pride, is unique in the world and in history" (Frey-W outers, 1980, p. 4). W hat is further interesting to note, is that according to him , the EC has "firm ly com m itted [itself] to the dynam ics of cooperation" (Ibid.).

For the m om ent, this statem ent will be left uncom m ented. The following of this section will trace the developm ent cooperation between the EC and the developing countries back to its origins, and will provide the reader with the circum stances under which the different trade regim es of the EC have developed, up to the point of now where we can speak of a "pyram id of trade preferences" (EC, 1995, p. 7). The m ain trade regim es in this pyram id consist of the Cotonou Agreem ent and the GSP schem e of the European Union. The Cotonou Agreem ent evolved out of the association system of the EC. Other parts in the pyram id include M editerranean Agreem ents and agreem ents relating to least developed countries (EC, 1995, p.8).

This background will be instrumental in order to make a judgment on the point of whether trade policy of the EU has been in cooperation with developing countries.

EC Associationism and the GSP scheme of the EC

At the inception of the Treaty of Rome in 1957 decolonization was still in its infancy, and indeed, not really foreseen by the European colonial powers (Grilli, 1993, p. 4). At the time of the negotiation at Bretton Woods in 1945 France and Great Britain tried to find ways to maintain and consolidate their empires (Brown, 2000, p. 369). This attitude had not fundamentally changed one decade later, when France negotiated with five other European countries the Treaty of Rome, which was to become the founding treaty of the European Economic Community. This is so because France made signing of the Treaty dependent upon the inclusion of the provision that its colonial territories were to be included in the free trade area of the Community. As the other countries did not want to abandon the European project, they accepted. Thus, the Treaty of Rome provided with part IV, which covered association of overseas countries and territories, the start of EC associationism. Of course, this association was unilateral and the colonial territories could play no part in the negotiations.

In the ensuing years, decolonization proceeded faster than was thought. This meant that the independent countries were no longer bound by the provisions of the Treaty of Rome. Thus, a new form of association needed to be found. The former colonial territories still had an interest in association, as they were still dependent on Europe in an economic sense. One could also argue that they had no other choice than to seek a new agreement with Europe, as their colonial heritage still kept them tied to Europe. For example, most of their products were destined for export markets located in Europe (Grilli, 1993, p.5). Coalesced into the Associated African and Malagasy States (AAMS), the 18 African states concluded with the six EC member states the Yaoundé Convention that was to become effective in 1964 and last until 1969. The second Yaoundé Convention, which was concluded in 1969 and lasted until 1975, was very similar to the first one. The parties to the Treaty Convention were the same, as well as its stated purposes, basic principles, main areas of cooperation and main instruments of cooperation.[2] The principles on which the Conventions were based were reciprocity and non-discrimination, as well as equality of partnership.

Ellen Frey-Wouters, who studied the Lomé Convention and its impact, agrees with what was mentioned before by stating that the initial EEC association in the

Treaty of Rome "reflected the intention of some to continue the old relation on the same basis" (1980, p.5). She adds that the Yaoundé Conventions did introduce some changes away from this unequal relationship, but in essence did not fundamentally alter it (Ibid.). The following Lomé Convention, which took effect in 1975, was hailed by many observers as they saw in it the incorporation of the beginnings of a more fundamental change (Frey-Wouters, 1980, pp.2-3). It is clear that this Convention was also influenced by the colonial past. However, it is less clear whether this Convention did constitute a breakthrough for the developing countries; a first step in the march towards an international economic order that is tailored to their development needs (Frey-Wouters, 1980, p.5). A clearer assessment of the nature of this Convention necessitates an analysis of the broader environment under which the Lomé Convention was negotiated. The following paragraphs will shed light on the international economic environment.

The above mentioned principles of the Yaoundé Conventions were basically in line with the trade orthodoxy of the post-war international economic order. The General Agreement on Tariffs and Trade was the body that was created after the Second World War, and its trade rules required reciprocity and non-discrimination by the contracting parties (Grilli, 1993, p.138). It was a body that was created by the industrialized countries, and the developing world argued that its principles favoured the industrialized world. The developing world was critical of the free trade enshrined in GATT because in order to exploit free trade some conditions must be present. The "internal deficiencies and basic economic weakness" of developing countries made it difficult for developing countries to adapt and thereby profit from free trade (Grilli, 1993, pp.138-139). The broader argument is that global trade relations governed by GATT are in essence rules that are written for "trading partners of comparable strength" (Brinkhorst, 1977, p.9). These were some of the reasons why developing countries started to demand a reconfiguration of the existing international economic order. Due to decolonization the developing countries were in the majority in the UN General Assembly. They succeeded in establishing the UN Conference on Trade and Development (UNCTAD), which should become the means to advance towards a "New International Economic Order" (NIEO). The Conferences were held every four years, with the first Conference in 1964.

The demands of the developing world during these Conferences met strong resistance by Western countries. However, as a consequence of UNCTAD II, the

13

developed world gave in to some pressures by allowing the establishment of the Generalized System of Preferences (GSP). These rules were first contradictory to the GATT rules, and therefore, in 1971, GATT granted the contracting parties a waiver from the most-favoured nation rule (MFN) (EC, 1995, p.9). This allowed industrialized countries to develop a GSP scheme, in which they can give preferential treatment to developing countries. Since the introduction of the GSP scheme of the EC, the main beneficiaries have been developing countries of Asia and Latin America. These are those countries that do not fall under the other preferential treatments of the EU, such as the Cotonou Agreement and others.

In the debates between developed and developing world about a NIEO that revolved around the UN Conferences on Trade and Development, Frey-Wouters identifies three stages. The stages bear the following titles and covered the following time periods: "The old international economic order" (1964–1973), "the Third World challenge" (October 1973-December 1974) and "the promise of cooperation" (January 1975-May 1976). What becomes evident is that there were times when the developed world found itself under growing pressure. This was strongest in the second stage. During that period the developing countries had also enormous bargaining power. Not only because the developing countries acted as a united front, but also because their demands came at a time when the developed world faced an "enduring global crisis" (Frey-Wouters, 1980, p.223). This crisis manifested itself in inflation, the breakdown of the international monetary system and the rise of raw materials prices. Especially the member states of the EC found themselves in a situation where they had to fear for the secure supply of raw materials. The sense of urgency is captured quite well in the words of French president Valerie Giscard d'Estaing, who predicted a "Europe of penury", partly because of a lack of resources.[3]

Consequently, the European countries saw itself forced to grant some concessions to the South in order to ward off the "threat of commodity power" (Grilli, 1993, p.41). These concessions were provided under the Lomé Convention. Therefore, only the group of developing countries that was party to that convention was able to benefit: the African, Caribbean and Pacific Group of States (ACP). The United Kingdom wanted, in the event of accession to the EC, to include their former colonial territories in a new association treaty.[4] Thus, the group of developing countries that were party to the convention was enlarged. Important for their negotiation power was that these different states coalesced in the ACP, and had one spokesman during their

14

negotiations. The provisions of the Lomé Convention were indeed relatively beneficial, and introduced some new features into the world trading system (Frey-Wouters, 1980, p.36). However, it can be argued that these benefits were part of a strategy to keep the situation under control (Frey-Wouters, 1980, p.7). It must be borne in mind that the European countries sought a means to ensure the secure supply of raw materials at a time when their economies were in great trouble. The ACP countries could provide them with the raw materials needed, and the Community's development policy was the means to safeguard the security of its supplies (Grilli, 1993, p. 49). Thus, their short-term concessions must be seen in the broader picture of trying to avoid long-range consequences that could occur in the case of failed confrontations (Frey-Wouters, 1980, p.7).

In conclusion, there is some reason to derive from the action pursued by the EC countries that the relatively remarkable, tolerating stance towards the ACP states in the Lomé Convention can be seen as the result of the urgency facing the EC countries at that time. Such an assessment stands in contrast to what has been said about the Lomé Convention from the side of the EC, and in particular by Mr. Cheysson (see above). What further supports such an argumentation is the fact that the first Yaoundé Convention has met the criticism of the associated countries. However, in the absence of an emergency situation, the EC did not give in to pressures and introduced the second Yaoundé Convention mainly unchanged. This can be regarded as further evidence of the fact that the EC does not commit itself to the "dynamics of cooperation" (Frey-Wouters, 1980, p.4) when it does not feel urged to do so.

The debates about NIEO also provide an opportunity to assess how the international economic order will be shaped as long as the developed world is its arbiter. In defence of the existing international economic order, state officials of the developed world voiced their conviction in the belief of the current order (Frey-Wouters, 1980, pp.221-225). For example, it came to the fore that economic stability of the industrialized world is a prerequisite, coming first before any moderation to the economic order can be considered (Frey-Wouters, 1980, p. 225). These statements can be seen as evidence of the fact that if not pressured, the EC countries will not modify their preferred policy.

Moreover, it is worth analyzing the ensuing conventions between the EC and the ACP. This is important as the economic environment was already drastically different five years after the first Lomé Convention. The EC countries regained the upper hand in the relationship, as some of the ACP countries, struggling with growing debts, clearly became dependent on loans of the international financial institutions, in which the West has most of the control. Thus, the dominance of the EC over the ACP was restored. The fact that the EC did not extend the provisions of the Lomé Convention so as to provide the ACP countries with more benefits, seems to confirm that the original, unique mechanisms in the Convention were largely adopted from a defensive position. Now that the EC countries were no longer threatened, they could restrict the negotiation of new conventions to managing the existing relationship, refraining from any new innovation. For example, it was argued that the third Lomé Convention was "void of real substance", foreseeing only in verbal concessions to the needs of developing countries (Grilli, 1993, p.38).

All in all, Lomé stagnated, as the EC countries saw no interest in adapting the Lomé model. More evidence can be found in the fact that the "functional scope or geographical reach" was not broadened (Grilli, 1993, p. 40). To sum up, it can be argued that the Lomé Convention I was indeed unique, but only in the sense that under "normal" circumstances of an unequal power relationship, the spirit of cooperation inherent in the first Convention is not replicable. It is quite revealing that some ACP leaders regarded Lomé I as a small "miracle" (Grilli, 1993, p.36). While shortly after the Lome Convention there were people who had wondered whether Lomé I would be a step towards a world trading system more conducive to the development of developing countries, one can be quite certain that they were disappointed by the stagnation of the Lomé model.

As a last point, it is worth noting that from the 1980s on, the EC countries knew to realize a shift in focus of Lomé. In contrast with earlier periods where the spirit of the Convention reflected the idea that external conditions needed to be improved in order to clear the way for development of the ACP states, the Conventions were more and more under the influence of the idea that the causes of low economic performance of the ACP states had a clear domestic dimension. In other words, it seems that the European countries came to share the belief that developing countries can only reap the benefits of preferential treatment if domestic policy makers create the right internal conditions that enable exports to become competitive (EC, 1995, p.25). Further evidence of the same trend is to be seen in the fact that the EU has assisted structural adjustment programmes in their dealings with developing countries (Langan, 2009). In other words, it has adopted the same policy stance towards developing countries as the international financial institutions – the World Bank and the IMF. For example, Lomé IV and IV/ii foresaw in economic and political conditionality (Brown, 2000, p.368). Two scholars that are leaning towards Marxism bring it to the point: "The evolution of the Lomé and Cotonou Agreements has complemented the global shift to neoliberal accumulation" (Nunn et al., 2004, p. 227). Notwithstanding the fact that there is certainly some truth behind the claim that amelioration of external conditions does not necessarily lead to better export performances without setting the right internal conditions (see also Szirm ai, 1994, p. 421), the argument can be made that by doing so the European countries knew to avoid making further concessions to the South. As we have seen, the concessions towards the ACP countries in the exceptional first Lomé Convention were granted only reluctantly, and hesitantly. As many noted, Lomé I was to be seen only as a first step towards a more just international economic order (Brinkhorst, 1977, p.7). Therefore, we can follow that there was a need to further lift the external constraints that are hampering the development of ACP countries, and that the European countries could not rightfully claim that attention needed to shift completely towards the internal dimension.

Chapter III: An Analysis of Preferential Treatment by the EU: Preferences that matter?

This section will put the focus on answering the following question: To what extent have the trade policies conducted by the EU contributed to the external constraints which hamper the development of developing countries? In order to provide an answer to that question it will mainly be analyzed whether the trade regimes have had a positive effect on the export performance of developing countries. Export earnings form an important part in the development process. In general, exports form a larger part of gross domestic product (GDP) for developing countries than for developed countries. The ratio of trade to GDP was 0.27 in 1963, increasing to 0.46 in 1980 (Faber, 1990, p. 11). The Newly Industrialized Countries (Singapore, Taiwan, Hong Kong, South Korea) have shown that exports can pave the way towards becoming an industrialized country.

Regarding the issue from some distance, one can ask, why is it that international trade forms an important part for the study of economic growth of developing countries? The importance of international trade becomes clear through an assessment of the consequences of a closed economy. Indeed, the world has seen an attempt of developing countries to limit the amount of trade with the developed world. This was in the 1950s and 1960s when the policy recommendation of import-substitution-industrialization was followed by many states of the South. The belief that international trade is a manifestation of colonial rule and foreign domination also gave impetus to this policy (Faber, 1990, p.29). However, this experience turned out to be quite costly, thus illustrating the developing world that they cannot avoid trade relations with the developed world (Faber, 1990, p.29). The fact that there are no viable alternatives to achieve economic growth may be seen as a tragic destiny. This is so because developing countries that become part of the world trading system will inevitably face competitors of unequal strength. The more dominant members of the trade system have the power to influence trade relations (Faber, 1990, p.6). Thus, it becomes important to evaluate to what extent developing countries efforts at development are externally constrained by the actions of more dominant states, such as the states forming part of the EU.

Needless to say, international trade, not only because of the benefits trade produces, has a distributive effect of the power of different actors in the international system (Faber, 1990, p. 7). More powerful states are in a position to manage the "behaviour of other states by direction or by threats, or by using their influence in the drawing up of rules" (Faber, 1990, p. 6). Therefore, it is quite logical to assume that development cooperation of the EU towards ACP states as well as other forms of trade relations, such as the GSP of the EU, do not "constitute some kind of technical or apolitical endeavour" (Brown, 2000, p.368).

One can see how this manifests itself in practice in the creation of the Bretton Woods institutions, which have been supported since their creation by the economically dominant nations of the West. The creation of these institutions can be regarded as an example of influencing the behaviour of other states by direction. Applying a Marxist perspective allows us to detect how this system ensures relatively more benefits from the world trade system for the dominant economies. Making developing countries play along the rules of the liberal economic order is in the interest of the hegemon and the dominant economies in at least two areas. Firstly, free trade is profitable for the dominant economies because their economies are more competitive as they are able to produce their products the most cheaply. Secondly, in a free trade situation developing countries need to export more of their raw materials as their industrial products cannot compete with those of the developed economies. This is in the interest of the North as more exports of raw materials means that the price of them decreases (Hobden et al, 2008, p.152).

As was mentioned, developing countries have discovered the bias of a world trade system based on free trade, which furthermore must be reciprocal and non-discrimatory. As a consequence of their pressures, some alterations to the world trade system have been made. Accordingly, the question arises whether these modifications were substantial in nature, thus reducing the imbalance of the system. In other words, have these modifications enhanced the opportunities of developing countries? This section will pass along two types of preferential treatments that the EU has assured to developing countries: the association agreements with the ACP group of states and the EU scheme of GSP.

A part of the EU-ACP agreements that is worth analyzing is industrial cooperation. It was first paid attention to in the Yaoundé Convention. The preamble stated the goals of furthering industrialization of the associated states as well as diversifying their economies (Grilli, 1993, p. 28). However, in reality, the EC rather opposed any efforts to build up processing facilities in developing countries. This can also be seen in the fact that the aid flows to developing countries were mainly used for infrastructure investments, instead of providing stimulus for "plans of a directly productive and industrial character" (Frey-Wouters, 1993, p. 15). During the negotiations of the first Lomé Convention, the ACP countries also demanded that they get assistance for the promotion of industrialization. They succeeded in including some promising clauses about industrial cooperation in the treaty. The provisions include "the development of infrastructures connected with industrialization [...]; contributions to the setting up of manufacturing industries and especially the processing of local raw materials; industrial training schemes in Europe and the ACP countries; measures for providing access to technology and its adaptation to local needs" and more (Frey-Wouters, 1980, p. 58).

It can be seen that the clauses are quite broad, and that the EC countries have committed themselves to quite some substantial cooperation. Although it shows that Lomé I has paid increased attention to industrial cooperation, it did not go as far as many ACP states would have liked (Grilli, 1993, p. 31). Moreover, the success of industrial cooperation will to a large extent depend on the energy that EC countries will invest into the implementation of these provisions. Besides, this is not only true for the provision of Lomé I relating to industrial cooperation (Brinkhorst, 1977, p.11). An evaluation of implementation efforts of the provisions of Lomé I and the succeeding association treaties would be very valuable for the present study, but would, unfortunately, go beyond the scope of it. Nevertheless, some remarks can be made. According to Grilli, the industrial cooperation clauses were mainly verbal statements, that later proved to be missing necessary action. Grilli adds that a factor which makes industrial cooperation always difficult is its nature. For example, transfer of technology is a field that takes place at the firm level, and is therefore beyond the influence of governments (1993, pp.31–32). Reaping the benefits of industrial cooperation, as well as of other advantages incorporated in the treaty was further frustrated by the "balance of political and economic power within the association", as well as by the "procedure of consultations under the Conventions" (Frey-Wouters, 1980, p. 15). Moreover, there are people who have reacted negatively to Lomé I, maintaining that through a "new and subtle kind of subjugation of the ACP states" their path towards industrialization and diversification of their economies is hampered (Frey-Wouters, 1980, p. 15).

Now, let us first turn to an elaboration of the GSP scheme of the EU, after which an examination of its provisions will follow. The GSP scheme is autonomous, meaning that the EU decides over its character unilaterally, entailing that negotiations do not take place. The EU does regularly ask the beneficiary countries of Latin America and Asia for their opinion, both bilaterally and in UNCTAD, but in the end it has the authority to decide the nature and content of its scheme unilaterally (EC, 1995, p. 9). As many states of the African continent are part of the ACP countries, their preferential treatment is governed by the association agreements (of which the Cotonou agreement is the latest), and they therefore do not fall under the GSP scheme. In principal, they were legally entitled to profit from the provisions of the GSP scheme, but they do not do so as the association agreements give them better preferential treatment.

The GSP scheme foresees in the reduction of tariff quotas, the amount of the reduction being dependent on the "sensitivity" of the imported product as well as the "development index" of exporting countries (Moore, 2001, p. 285). "Sensitivity" of the imported products include four categories, ranging from "very sensitive" products, "sensitive" products, "semi-sensitive" products and "non-sensitive" products. The first category is relevant for many agricultural products, textiles, clothing and ferro-alloys. For these products, the preferential rate of duty is 85 per cent of the most favoured nation (MFN) duty, meaning that the margin of preference is 15 percent. The preferential duties of the other categories are, respectively, 70 per cent, 35 per cent, and zero (Ibid.). Regarding textiles and clothing, the EU and other developed countries were cautious as they faced increasing competition from developing countries in this area. This is why there are some additional provisions made in the framework of the Multi Fibre Arrangement (MFA) that regulate GSP treatment for developing countries regarding textiles and clothing (Blokker, 1990, p. 185). As a general note, it is obvious that product coverage under the GSP scheme is limited and that the margin of preference was often quite small. The limited preferential customs treatment expresses itself in that it does not cover non-tariff barriers (Stordel, 1990, p. 67).

What seems to be striking is the fact that imports of the ACP group of states do not form a great part of the overall imports of the EU. In 1980, imports of this group amounted to 16 per cent of the EU's total imports. This decreased to the amount of 9 per cent in 1993 (EC, 1995, p. 15). What does this tell us given the background that preferential treatment under the association agreements is far more encompassing than under the GSP scheme? As imports from the ACP group form only a minor part of imports, it might be argued that the EU was only willing to give preferential treatment to a minority of developing countries. However, it was cautious in limiting the preferential treatment towards the larger group of developing countries. The EU was also intent not to erode the preferences of the ACP countries by keeping the GSP scheme limited (EC, 1995, p.7). One of the reasons it has brought forward for doing so is that ACP exports in agriculture and raw materials could not face the competition of other developing countries. Upon the inception of Lomé I it was already remarked that a significant step towards a more just international economic order needed to be complemented by similar measures towards the community of developing countries as a whole (Stordel, 1990, p.80).

Any discussion about the potential of developing countries to access the market of the EU must include the restriction of market access and the trade distortions caused by the Common Agricultural Policy of the EU (CAP). There are many critical voices claiming that the CAP is highly incoherent with the EU's development objectives. The CAP is harmful to the interests of the ACP countries, as in Lomé I the Community offered no preferential access for agricultural products "which fall directly or indirectly under the [CAP]" (Dodoo et al, 1977, p 37).

In addition, demands are made for abolition of some provisions of the CAP by developing countries in the Doha Development Round, which is the current trade-negotiation round of the WTO. The talks have stalled because the developed world, and especially the EU, does not agree with demands to change their level of agricultural support and protection (Matthews, 2008, p.382). At the moment the EU does not show itself ready to reduce the level of subsidies it pays to EU farmers, upholding a situation of unfair competition with agricultural products of developing countries.

The present chapter was designed to determine the degree to which EU trade policy negatively influences or constrains the development of countries in the South. In order to do so this evaluation covered the following aspects of EU trade policy that have an impact on the South: The GSP scheme of the EU, the association agreements of the EU with the ACP group of states, and the CAP. Concluding, it can be said that only the CAP has a direct negative influence on developing countries. Its provisions still make it difficult for developing countries to profit from the comparative advantage they enjoy with regard to agricultural products. The preferential treatment included in the GSP as well as in the association agreements excludes products that fall under the protection of the CAP. Without all-encompassing preferential treatment, EU trade policy therefore comes down to constraining economic development in the South.

Conclusion

The present study was designed to determine the effect that external causes have on the development prospects of developing countries. In particular, the study set out to test the assumptions of dependency theory about how external causes work out. In order to do so the trade relations between the EU and developing countries have been analyzed. One of the more significant findings to emerge from this study is that the trade relations of the EU bear a clear connection with the past. The colonial past is especially evident in the association agreements the EU has adopted with its former colonial territories. Many of the ACP countries formerly belonged to one of the European empires. In addition, this study has shown that the EU has only reluctantly allowed modifications to the international economic order. Modifications to the external environment were only granted if the countries of the EU found themselves under considerable pressure. Thus, this study suggests that the external factors will not change for the better unless political action on the side of the developing countries is taken.

The results of this study reveal that the association agreements of the EU resulted in only limited efforts to follow demands made by developing countries. This was especially the case in the field of industrial cooperation. Diversification of their economies was rather discouraged than supported. Moreover, it was shown that without a push for reform and further concessions from the side of the developing countries, the EU countries lacked an interest in widening or improving the association agreements. This was also a consequence of the decrease in negotiation power of the developing countries.

Furthermore, this study has found that preferential treatment of the EU towards developing countries has clear limits. So-called "sensitive" products are excluded from preferential treatment, or only enjoy a minimal margin of preference. This is especially the case for agricultural products because they form a threat to agricultural products that fall under the CAP.

It can be concluded that some of these findings confirm the assumptions of dependency theory on the importance of external causes. The trade relations between the EU and developing countries can be seen as partly reflecting relations between satellite underdeveloped and developed metropolitan countries.

N otes

[1] The term s European U nion' (EU), U nion' or Europe' are used interchangeably. The term s European Econom ic Com m unity' (EEC) or European Com m unity' (EC) are only used w hen em phasising the historical dim ension (pre–M aastricht era).

[2] The stated purpose of the Yaoundé Convention w as: "Furthering the industrialization of the associated States, and the diversification of their econom ies" (Pream ble). The m ain instrum ents of cooperation w ere free–trade areas betw een EC and each associate. Furtherm ore, EC aid w as a m ain instrum ent. N ext to trade, another m ain area of cooperation w as right of establishm ent of firm s and individuals (G rilli, 1993, pp.28,29).

[3] H is w ords w ere: "... this is no passing perturbation. It is the revenge of Europe for the nineteenth century ... Europe is in decline, a decline in population and an im poverishm ent in resources. The Europe w e have to build now is a Europe of penury" (Frey–W outers, 1983, p 223).

[4] The U nited K ingdom , as w ell as Ireland and D enm ark, acceeded to the EC in 1973.

List of references

Amin, Samir. 1994. The origin and development of underdevelopment. In Rajani Kanth (Ed.) *Paradigms in Economic Development: Classic Perspectives, Critiques, and Reflections.* M.E.Sharpe.

Blokker, Niels. 1990. The Common Commercial Policy of the EEC and Developing Countries: The Legal Framework. In Gerrit Faber (Ed.) *Trade Policy and Development: The Role of Europe in North-South Trade; A Multidisciplinary Approach.* Universitaire Pers Rotterdam.

Brinkhorst, L.J. 1977. Lomé and Further. In Frans A M.Alting von Geusau (Ed.) *The Lomé Convention and a New International Economic Order.* A W.Sijhoff.

Browett, John. 1985. The Newly Industrializing Countries and Radical Theories of Development.*World Development* 13,no 7:789-803.

Brown, Chris.1985.Development and Dependency. In Margot Light and Arthur John Richard Groom (Eds.) *International relations: a handbook of current theory.* London:Pinter.

Brown, William.2000.Restructuring North-South Relations: ACP-EU Development Co-operation in a Liberal International Order. *Review of African Political Economy,* no 85:367-383.

Chase-Dunn, Christopher. 1975. The Effects of International Economic Dependence on Development and Inequality: A Cross-National Study. *American Sociological Review* 40,no 6:720-738.

Clapham , Christopher. 1996. Governmentality and Economic Policy in Sub-Saharan Africa.*Third World Quarterly* 17,no 4:809-824.

DeVault, James M. 1996. Political Pressure and the U.S. Generalized System of Preferences. *Eastern Economic Journal* 22, no 1: 35-46.

Disney, Nigel. 1977. Review Essays: Accumulation On a World Scale. *Critical Sociology*, no 7: 124-128.

Dodoo, C. And R. Kuster. 1977. The Road to Lomé. In Frans A M. Alting von Geusau (Ed.) *The Lomé Convention and a New International Economic Order.* A W. Sijhoff.

European Commission. 1995. *Trade Relations between the European Union and the Developing Countries.* Office for Official Publications of the European Communities.

Faber, Gerrit. 1990. Introduction. In Gerrit Faber (Ed.) *Trade Policy and Development: The Role of Europe in North-South Trade; A Multidisciplinary Approach.* Universitaire Pers Rotterdam.

Faber, Gerrit. 1990. Trade and Economic Development. In Gerrit Faber (Ed.) *Trade Policy and Development: The Role of Europe in North-South Trade; A Multidisciplinary Approach.* Universitaire Pers Rotterdam.

Foster-Caster. 1976. From Rostow to Gunder Frank: Conflicting Paradigms in the Analysis of Underdevelopment. *World Development* 4, no 3: 167—180.

Frank, André Gunder. 1994. The Development of Underdevelopment. In Rajani Kanth (Ed.) *Paradigms in Economic Development: Classic Perspectives, Critiques, and Reflections.* M E. Sharpe.

Frey-Wouters, Ellen. 1980. *The European Community and the Third World: The Lomé Convention and its Impact.* Praeger Publishers.

Grilli, Enzo R. 1993. *The European Community and the Developing Countries.* Cambridge University Press.

Hobden, Stephen and Richard Wyn Jones. 2008. Marxist Theories of International Relations. In John Baylis, Steve Smith, Patricia Owens (eds.) *The Globalization of World Politics*. Oxford University Press.

Hout, W il. 1993. *Capitalism and the Third World: development, dependence and the world system*. Aldershot, Hants.

Hunt, Diane. 1989. *Economic Theories of Development: An Analysis of Competing Paradigms.* Harvester Wheatsheaf.

Langan, Mark. 2009. ACP-EU Normative Concessions from Stabex to Private Sector Development: Why the European Union's Moralised Pursuit of a Deep' Trade Agenda is Nothing New' in ACP-EU Relations. *Perspectives on European Politics and Society* 10, no.3:416-440.

Moore, Lynden. 2001. Developments in Trade and Trade Policy. In Mike Artis and Frederick Nixson (Eds.) *The Economics of the European Union: Policy and Analysis.*

Nunn, Alex and Sophia Price. 2004. Managing Development: EU and African Relations through the Evolution of the Lomé and Cotonou Agreements. *Historical Materialism* 12, no 4:203-230.

Matthews, Alan. 2008. The European Union's Common Agricultural Policy and Developing Countries: the Struggle for Coherence. *Journal of European Integration* 30, no 3:381– 399.

Rittberger, Volker and Bernard Zangl. 2006. *International Organization: Polity, Politics and Policies.* Palgrave Macmillan.

Sapir, André and Lars Lundberg. 2008. The US. Generalized System of Preferences and its Impacts. In Robert E. Baldwin and Anne O. Krueger (Eds.) *Structure and Evolution of recent U. S. Trade Policy.* University of Chicago Press.

Schiffer, Jonathan. 1981. The Changing Post-war Pattern of Development: The Accumulated Wisdom of Sam ir Am in. *World Development* 9, no 6:515 – 537.
Smith, B.C. 2009. *Understanding Third World Politics: Theories of Political Change and Development.* Palgrave Macmillan.

Sm ith, Sheala. 1980. The Ideas of Sam ir Am in: Theory or Tautology? *Journal of Development Studies* 17, no 1: 5 – 20.

Sm ith, Tony. 1979. The U nderdevelopm ent of D evelopm ent Literature: The Case of D ependency Theory. *World Politics* 31, no 2: 247–288.

Stordel, H arry. 1977. T rade Cooperation: P references in the Lom é Convention, The G eneralized System of P references and the W orld T rade System . In F rans A M . A lting von G eusau (Ed.) *The Lomé Convention and a New International Economic Order.* A W . Sijhoff.

Szirm ai, A . 1994. *Ontwikkelingslanden: Dynamiek en Stagnatie.* W olters-N oordhoff G roningen.

YOUR KNOWLEDGE HAS VALUE